BEYOND BORDERS

BEYOND BORDERS

WILLIAM VINCENT

CONTENTS

CHAPTER 1

Introduction to Globalization

Globalization is a term that has come to attain such a prominent position in recent years that rarely any political or economic event does not hinge on it. It is being depicted as the force responsible for hastening widespread liberal reforms and introducing a new governance structure. The process has been around for many years and has affected the lives of everyone, one way or the other, including the production and consumption across the globe. One of the images of the globalized world is the triumph of capitalism with its technological progression. One of the main attributes of the globalization wave is the liberalization of trade which has been the driver of globalization, and trade liberalization has not only a visible effect on the global economy but also on other fronts.

Globalization denotes a process of increasing interconnectedness. For an adept purist, it is more than simply increasing trade and capital flows. It can be broadly defined as a world in action or movement. This ensures that everything spreads from place to place through the movement of people, capital, information, and property. In order to understand the consequences, one must examine closely the way in which that world is connected. The terms of the debate include both politics and perceptions encompassing what happens and people's view of what happens. What seems clear to one side might seem unintelligent to the opposite side. The study of globalization is replete with examples of how volatile the issue has become and the direction and source of hostility from many quarters towards the process.

Defining Globalization

The processes of globalization have been analyzed from the lenses of diverse conceptual paradigms – political, economic, and sociological – which converge around power. Many scholars have underscored the association between economic growth since countries became increasingly open to global competition. Others have emphasized the importance of the communication, transportation, and technology revolutions. The latter have assisted the narrowing of the physical distances between countries; and raised the degree of international dispersion and international economic integration, supporting the greater mobility of people, goods, and money.

Globalization is a very powerful but at the same time a nebulous concept. It can be undefined or over-specified, making it a task to identify reasonable units of analysis. However, a working definition should capture the processes and constructs without exaggeration. It is best to make the definition as simple as possible but complex enough to involve the processes tied to the shift towards, on the one hand, pyramidal strengthening of the global marketing, or integration; and on the other hand, the broader spread of political, economic, social, and technological networks. These networks blur the linear ties between territorial boundaries allowing the centers of power to focus upon the individual and global elite.

Historical Context

After about three post WWII decades of increasing policy co-operation, major economies reintroduced floating exchange rates, trade protectionism and stricter capital controls from the 1970s onwards. Sinuous, perhaps inevitable, effects of a deepened global economic situation include increasing unemployment, lower wages and an increase in social exclusion. These surprisingly broad impacts of intensified international economic relationships in developed economies might perhaps have not been a shock had some putative meanings of 'globalization' been taken to better task a decade ago. Then (as now), individuals are importing and purchasing more from abroad compared to the 'homogeneous', 'unsophisticated', 'narrow nationalistic' mansions (countries) they resided in some years ago. Small and large enterprises are hit by shocks from the 5-6 payers selling to domestic markets from abroad.

Historically, the world has gone through various phases of globalization, which were often followed by significant drawbacks or retrenchments. Before World War One (WWI), a high degree of global economic integration was maintained. One great example of this integration is trade flows: in this era, import and export volumes were as much as 60% of the world's industrial output compared to only 22.5% in 1990. Moreover, capitalism and government policy for international cooperation subsequently came under fire; the world experienced communism in the former Soviet Union and the satellite states, while other countries adopted protectionism and economic nationalism. Internationally, a protectionist trade policy stance was adopted in the form of bilateral and regional trade negotiations, overtaking the dominant multilateral trade negotiations occurring under GATT (General Agreements on Tariffs and Trade).

CHAPTER 2

Economic Aspects of Globalization

In a business setting, money regards design aesthetics or cultural idiosyncrasies as a mere commercial operational burden. Once the financial clock turns in sync with the value of each hour for a locality, businesses are poised to enter a materialistic vertical take-off. In group, the decisive event in a window of opportunity for rapid business expansion was the political decision to embrace capitalism. Freedom to make a living, probably in a capitalist competitive context, is a legitimate claim. Economic resources are distributed differently according to political choices affecting the economy, but its ownership is what will set the clock running again against any company that fails to grab the opportunity to enter the global economy.

Globalization is the buzzword that seems to be the first option whenever anybody is interested in how the planet is connected and affected by issues or aspects that denote a global reach. Today, business borders are not fixed, and large companies (and even small companies) are setting up manufacturing plants, distribution facilities, and service centers wherever they receive the best economic reception: the cost of doing business is what prompts the process. Profitability is the bottom line driving every corporate negotiation within the international sphere -- that is also the last word that sums up the globalization phenomenon. The apparently strong links lacing production, distribution, sales and even capital resources are the economic precondition that exposes the deep relationships that firms have with the markets they intend to serve. Governments are aware that tolerating a damagingly high cost of doing business stands as a hurdle of death for favored firms and jobs, but they are also reluctant to expose it to some anti-globalization movements sponsored by labor groups and environmental organizations.

Trade and Investment

Trade and specialization among nations enable people to make the most of their different endowments and create an efficient system of production and distribution. As early as 1817, David R. Ricardo had already offered the idea in his On the Principles of Political Economy and Taxation. Subsequent contributions and newfound compensation principles allowed the extension of these simple truths and led to a major field in economic thought: nations trading among themselves without any assistance from foreign countries could reach a collective optimum, it was believed. Once trade improved the use of the world's resources, the doctrine of comparative advantage was picked as one of the bolts of universal liberal merit. Then the Industrial Revolution came and urban markets expanded. Nations started interacting among themselves by trading the simple goods and services they produced. The only appropriate role for foreign trade was providing them with goods that were not available where they lived, it was believed. At the end of the 19th century, British economist Alfred Marshall would finally introduce a distinction between foreign trade and entrepreneurship. The "adventurer-booty" idea of explorative capitalism returned to its rightful place: people participated in global trade because it was profitable to do so.

Almost without exception, the quick response to the term "globalization" is an association with remarkable business and economic developments. That is, the agents typically associated with the concept are companies (not countries), and the developments in question have to do with expanding international trade and relations, roaring worldwide financial flows, as well as an increasing movement of technology and investment across national borders. Indeed, what has come to be known as "globalization" is essentially economic in nature. At the heart of the entire process are the worldwide financial and business markets and how people have been utilizing them. Perhaps the most impressive measure of the globalization of economic activities refers to business linkages - spanning trade, investment, and finance.

Labor Markets

In the short run, policies can affect the force of these effects. Increased globalization need not lead to increased income inequality, and firms can respond to competitive losses by finding and exploiting niche comparative advantage, in the process raising the profitability of the firm and thereby raising the wages of their employees. Openness to the world trading system has been an established fact of the economist's toolkit. Nevertheless, these are first-best policies. Given political pressures and the constraining factors that damage government credibility, the adoption of these policies may be more difficult. So, the political economy of trade intervention is clearly sometimes dominated by narrow interest groups, but not always. It is also pertinent to note that there seem to be good reasons to believe that international trade shall continue to grow due to the convergence dynamics of globalization.

Global competition involves several distinct types of activities that produce two different concerns regarding wages in labor markets. First, domestic labor markets are more directly linked now than ever before to other countries' labor markets. All labor markets reflect the impacts of supranational policy. Just as we will discuss in the next chapter how national policies are leaching out as the rules of the trading activity conducted by global citizens is expanded, with direct impacts on any economic unit, firms (and their shareholders) are only one of these, the incomes of workers are increasingly linked to this globalization. Second, this connects to a phenomenon known as increased wage dispersion or increased income inequality. A third effect widely reported in the world's literature is that of a downward set of pressures on wages resulting from the falling profitability of globalized firms forced into price competition with one another. This pressure has then been translated into non-wage calls on workers, such spending choice is not added to the value of the wage compensation package. These calls mean that trades unions and firms are unlikely to accept such patterns in low-wage countries such as China and Bangladesh, and indeed workers may actively resist such calls.

For centuries, labor economists have observed and wondered about why wages differ across workers in different locations, even within a single country. The answers to this question are varied, initially premised solely on the spatial differentiation of costs. So labor can migrate from low- to high-wage areas. Labor economists have known for more than a century that wages are lower in the U.S. Deep South than in the industrial Northeast. Wages are also lower in widely dispersed rural China than in coastal cities where booming export activity is drawing hundreds of millions of workers. Differences in characteristic value contribute to wage differences. The market price of a worker, like that of any input, reflects the value of the service the input can provide. Nowadays, economic analysis has extended the range of contributing characteristics and linked the rewards of such financial rewards to education, experience, and occupation-specific qualifications.

Cultural Dimensions of Globalization

Transnationalizers such as global mass media have made the icons and myths of today's popular culture (or "small" culture) endemic to world-wide audiences. Although initiated, financed, and distributed by powerful entities based in wealthy or industrially developing states, what are commonly perceived as "American" or "Euro/Anglo" cultural products are increasingly global, if by "global" we mean widely distributed, recognized, and influential across many societies. Encounters with these ideas and artifacts frequently result in sometimes subtle, sometimes serious modifications of the receiving societal culture. Such influences also stir reactions of resistance, or at least of protectionist deflection and adaptation in the receiving society. Reactions to the cultural intrusions have led to embracing local-mediated speech and communication styles or legitimately peculiar languages. The content of the new transnational culture is poised to weaken both nation-state control of domestic original media and intrastate control, designed to maintain and protect the local connectedness desired by substate elements or minorities.

Globalization has cultural consequences; this is true at the societal, national, and also the global level. We summarized research findings by stating that globalization processes promote differentiations and integrations of cultural spheres around the planet. This statement reflects a paradox that raises intriguing questions about how globalization processes of econocultural transnationalization influence the state of cultural differences in a world whose population has much easier access to alternative cultural goods and ideas from other cultures. When markets promote the spread of global cultural differences, what happens to local, indigenous cultural differences? Cultural processes of hybridization point to new mixtures, entanglements, or elements of cultural elements.

Cultural Exchange and Influence

In addition to the changing appearance of the physical landscape, as in the case of fast food chains, there are more qualitative changes that occur when cultures mix. For example, on their way to class, a Chinese engineer listens to the CD of a cowboy (Randy Travis), Vivaldi's The Four Seasons, and a rerun of the French musical Notre Dame de Paris. The engineer comes from a country known for heavy regulation of its media, and in giving examples of globalization, we determined that the items that had a significant global presence included the U.S. country-and-western singer Randy Travis, the Italian composer Antonio Vivaldi, and the French musical Notre Dame de Paris. As for the Chinese engineer's homeland, its harshest critics point to widespread restrictions of freedom and the widespread practice of a single party monopoly.

We begin our examination of globalization with the aspect that appears to be most positive, or most culturally enriching: the idea of globalism. Globalism refers to the growing integration of the world in terms of economics, politics, communications, and culture. Imagine if you will, that every person in the world has an invisible string attached to their culture; that these imaginary strings pull every culture together so that they merge into one single culture. Were we to sum up this idea in one word, we might use syncretism, a cultural trait that is syncretistic is one that demonstrates blending of forces. A fast-food hamburger is an example of syncretism. The hamburger is U.S. in origin, but it contains lettuce from France, peppers from Mexico or Spain, or tomatoes from Italy, spices from India, and meat from who knows where.

TECHNOLOGICAL INNOVATIONS AND GLOBALIZATION

Those who have access to information have the power to use that information. While it may be said that the world's sharing of knowledge has been on the increase, it still remains grossly skewed along economic lines. Many regions in underdeveloped countries have yet to experience firsthand the global phenomenon. Access requires the ability to communicate information as well as receive it. This means that in many cases, if a country is not among the first to adopt new technology, it will continuously remain a stranger to the benefits of that technology. It is therefore important that the barriers preventing the flow and sharing of information be kept low in order to maintain a level of openness in the global economy in the future.

Technological change and innovations have helped define the exchange of knowledge, attitudes, and ways of doing things, which in turn have contributed to both national and international economic, social, and cultural structures. Human creativity and information are now the core of the economy, with technology and know-how not limited to a particular group of professionals. Whether it be advances in information technology and e-commerce, biotechnology, the jet engine, the internal combustion engine, the spinning jenny, or new sources of energy, technological innovations always have been a chief source of not only new wealth and power, but also influence on the direction of globalization.

Information and Communication Technologies

The Internet connects all corners of the world and has suddenly become a powerful economic driver in virtually every nation, albeit to varying degrees. Information and Communication Technologies (ICT) have greatly facilitated the task of those analyzing the spread of the information society. ICT is responsible for the development of the national and international information society. Saner and Yiu, 1997, have emphasized the role of new ICT in cutting information and communication costs, increasing their global instantness, and allowing globally accessible files. These processes encourage the formation of trade networks leading to global economic integration. Enterprises no longer have to invest in large-scale in-house production of knowledge, and this has led to a significant acceleration in the international division of labor. It has also led to a mass expansion of the use of information services at a global level.

The first technological revolution was based on making more out of less, especially in mechanizing the work of humans and animals by employing water and wind power to drive machinery. The second technological revolution was based on making nothing out of everything, namely harnessing electricity to new technologies in telecommunication to operate far-flung and knowledge-intensive activities (including involving audio-visual means), industry using machines and chemicals on a mass scale, and rolling stock which could utilize oil as a fuel source. The third industrial revolution is based on micro-technology for the logical processing of information and communication technology for globalizing all sorts of transactions, be it in the sphere of financial markets, trade, or communication systems. Information that was earlier never communicated is today placed in the public domain, thanks to information explosion. The computer is a part and parcel of human life in the modern world and its decline is fraught with serious consequences for the world economy. The rich countries of Europe and the Americas have made the use of the computer part of the service structure of the industry's production process.

Globalization is a multidimensional process and technology is one of its key elements. Technology can be understood as the application of science to the solution of social problems. It is an arsenal of tools or elements to solve particular challenges facing human society. Technological literacy, therefore, is an understanding of the tools of society and the ability to harness those tools. Modernization and technological change are important stimulants of globalization; in fact, they accentuate the dimensions of economic, social, and environmental changes. The chief engines of globalization are rapid population growth, the industrial revolution, a combination of information and communication technology, and political globalization. The rapid development and diffusion of information and communication technology (ICT) is, however, the major driver of globalization.

CHAPTER 4

Political Implications of Globalization

A democratic state is supposed to reflect the interests of all its citizens but, with conventional politics powerless to prevent this growing economic polarization, angry, left-out majorities are electing new leaders who react by trying to avoid globalization. This is evident in many parts of the world and, in 1997, the trend contributed to more than 30 new elections in which failed politicians were ousted. The emergent leaders, with the clout of an angry electorate behind them, are demanding that political considerations take precedence over economic ones. The often-democratic elections over the last two years have introduced many radicals into office—some behaviorally—and outsiders are gaining power and demanding that domestic problems be allowed to take priority over the wishes of the international economic establishment.

The globalization of markets and production has enabled firms in some states to be very successful by producing globally competitive products at low cost. This success stems from access to a global pool of cheap labor and from trade and investment rules that enable firms to market their products globally with minimum trade barriers. As a few firms in a few countries become very successful, the disparities between the rich and the poor—among nations, and among people within nations—have grown sharply. The cost of living, relative to incomes, has risen in all countries, so that ordinary people expect that their children will have lower living standards than they have, and education, housing, and healthcare costs weigh more heavily as governments reduce their welfare and social services expenditures. For many, this is both tragic and unacceptable.

International Organizations and Governance

Some form of international organization lay behind almost all the successful models of the global economic order. This was true of the nineteenth century gold standard, which in many respects operated as a giant public financial policy cartel. It is even more evident in the neoliberal model of the global free trade system. Indeed, that model of globalization suggests that these organizations are in some ways a necessary condition for mutually beneficial globalization.

The trade-off between national sovereignty and global governance that I have discussed is associated with international organizations. They are both our means of global governance and our devices for pooling sovereignty. These organizations represent the tendency of states to try to create collective goods by managing outside of the state. Some of them also represent the failure of that tendency because they do little more than represent. International organizations represent the cooptation of nonstate actors into the state, and some of them represent the constraint imposed by these actors on states. Thus, their members are typically nation-states and typically international organizations are directed at creating or regulating international markets to ensure that they function well.

CHAPTER 5

Environmental Consequences

Clearly, competition for mobile factors of production, competition over immobile downstream adjustment costs, and simply a desire to avoid pollution are sources of leverage in developing such extraterritorial environmental leverage. The popular nature of these motivations renders troubling the absence of any formal regime for brokering such issues at the international level. Absent established ground rules of the game is presented frequently; absent uniform rules, such bargaining may give rise to an increased reliance on bilateral bargaining and ever complex web of preferential trading arrangements.

The most direct and visible effects of the world's increasing interdependence are those that manifest themselves in the natural environment. These consequences of expanding globalization began to appear even as the process was still in its relatively early stages. International debates on creating the infrastructure for managing global-level issues such as climate change and ozone depletion began in the 1980s. Concerns about the international spillover of environmental degradation led the United States and its Canadian and Mexican neighbors to the negotiation of the North American Agreement on

Environmental Cooperation (NAAEC) parallel to the North American Free Trade Agreement (NAFTA). Even some of the customary "club approach to multilateral negotiations has only modest effects on the policy of non-members.

Climate Change and Resource Depletion

The connections between climate change and resource scarcity have two strands: the traditional limits imposed on the exploitation of resources by human populations, and how the location of key resources such as fossil fuels influences world politics. Where fossil energy sources are situated, it underlies one part of the intense interest in the war-torn Middle East. Unlike the exploitative concerns, its significance lies in the power of the forces associated with these resources to shape political strategies by suppliers and to constrain the independence of the users. Such topics become supercharged in the kinetic world of climate change, echoing the minor skirmishes that the capacity to tax trade in wealthy industrialized countries caused with resource-poor emerging economies of the time. Bush called climate change 'Green Protectionism' and openly warned nations such as China and India against 'unfair treaty conditions' and 'punishing mandatory cap-and-trade' quotas. Other resource-rich economies, such as Russia, follow. Unsuccessful attempts to deflect such imports would provide a broad spectrum of the trade security link in the climate change debate, while demonstrating the increasing opposition to too much globalization in terms of too free trade that has emerged in the passage of Prime Minister Friedland.

Climate change will affect dimensions of globalization in unanticipated ways, altering access routes, contesting property rights, causing a shift in economic activities, generating refugees and migrants, and changing the distances across places. Climate changes affect the complexity of current global connections and therefore contribute to a rethinking of globalization, both frankly and imaginatively.

CHAPTER 6

Social Movements and Resistance to Globalization

The forces of globalization also have generated a powerful counter-globalization movement that reflects the expansion of civil society. The scale and reach of the alternative movement have surprised many, ranging from humanitarian protest at the World Trade Center's summit in 1999, to the setting up of alternative institutions and social forums. Social movements embark on various activities for change, and some even shape the structure of international society. Yet they are also internally stratified, and their clout remains limited. In addition, social movements often have trouble crystallizing coherent ideas, political strategies, and organizational structures, and can be accused of lack of vision, unrealistic goals, and centralized decision-making by some of their own members.

Social movements emerge in open public spaces, as citizens work to counteract the sense of alienation and integration that globalization can produce. The movement of people across and within borders is a tried-and-true method of asserting rights for many people, and a form of social and political protest against what may be seen as unjust or unfair rules by various global institutions. However, many experts maintain that it is not just people migration (low wage and temporary workers) that is at play, but a surge in transnational citizenship, rooted in the initiative of ordinary people. Both the internet and international migration have been seen to help create transnational communities; migration helps by fostering networks forging a wealth of cross-border ties that continue to nourish identification with historical or cultural territories.

Anti-Globalization Movements

There is also concern that globalization is a process where the rules are made by those who have the power and who will generally have a vested interest in protecting those industries and interests which are threatened by international competition. The market is still seen as the prime motivator in a globalized world and may not always deliver what is best for any given society. At a different level, those opposed to globalization also see it as a source of culture dilution as transnational corporations dominate the ever-widening range of media and entertainment services.

In response to globalization, there has also been the growth of anti-globalization movements both in the developed and developing world. They have challenged institutions such as the World Bank, the International Monetary Fund, and the World Trade Organization, which are seen as promoting a one-size-fits-all development formula to the rest of the world. While supporters of globalization emphasize its potential role in economic development and efficiency and that with appropriate measures, the costs can be minimized, the anti-globalization groups cite a range of social, political, and economic costs. Political and social concerns center upon the fear of countries losing control and acceptance of decisions imposed from outside, while economic costs in developed countries range from job loss in import-competing industries to falling wage levels, lower social and environmental standards, and lower government tax revenues.

CHAPTER 7

Globalization and Inequality

The advances in personal freedom and current living that are part of the globalization and innovation correlate. These technological advances make it possible for customers and employees to talk with the people who handle client services directly and informally without paying commission or airfare. Simultaneously, when driving off shareholders and traditional performance measures to allow employees to meet their own priorities, providers are increasingly supposed to be corporations. Both components are just looks at increasing demand for intrinsic benefits in the workplace, which increases with the standard calculated by data on stocks of the optimal effort intrinsic motivation and measures like community service or job purpose in the data of hiring markets, as mentioned in the introduction. Small and proficient global companies can initiate some of these shifts on their own and way ahead of regulators, moving in the direction of a world in which the globalization attractions win to be mutual.

Much of the often loud critique of globalization relates to growing inequality among people, within countries, and among countries: outputs of global economic forces that are to a large extent the results of government's and policymakers' choices. That is, inequality is not an unavoidable byproduct of globalization, but instead the result of decisions that governments, both featured and not, have taken to stand with or against their citizens. Broadly based benefits are achievable in an increasingly interconnected world economy; ebbs and flows in global integration have remarkable effects to change living standards within and across borders. The profile that is required to make sure that the broadening gains exist is not one that could be conjectured without evident, vocal, and organized skepticism about globalization.

Income Disparities

The idea that a rising tide lifts all boats does not hold true in a world of widely different starting points for the holders of capital. From the perspective of individual workers in developed and many developing countries, the potential benefits flowing from a global economic network reside in the forms of increasing consumer welfare, producer gains, and an increased choice of goods (as well as social and political gains). Seen from the perspective of the country itself, the international economy offers economic growth, capital formation, greater efficiency, and improved living standards. This assumption is based on the assumption that "however, in a welfare state, there may be a link between national wealth and the well-being of low-income groups as gains of world trade may be redistributed through higher state-provided resources."

Income disparities among individuals and inequality in the distribution of wealth are cited by many as factors leading to a backlash against the forces of globalization. As noted earlier, a central pillar of both classical and modern economic theory predicts that the world will experience improvements in overall economic welfare as international trade expands. This prediction serves as a justification for the changes in the economic institutions and policies of many countries designed to liberalize trade. However, many critics argue that while international capital and goods markets may be successful in promoting growth, that growth unevenly benefits a small proportion of the global population. Powerful economic actors such as transnational corporations and banks, aligned with the world's elite class, are seen as the main beneficiaries in the current system. The question of the impact of globalization on global income and wealth disparities, as well as on poverty, is thus central to the current debate about globalization.

CHAPTER 8

Case Studies on Globalization

After considering the role of the World Trade Organization, it was suggested that globalization may not work for everyone. There are many opponents to the theory, including anti-capitalists and environmentalists, who argue that globalization increases poverty and vulnerability rather than reducing it. Indeed, while globalization brings benefits for many, for others it is not easy to compete in the global market, and they do poorly from the extra competition brought about. School curricula often focus on a narrow range of impacts, which we frequently hear about. When thinking about globalization's role in the world, it is useful to look at the picture from a wider range of perspectives. That way we can put the controversies and debates of globalization in context and see what globalization truly does for the world.

This lesson pulled together information on the various impacts of globalization from several different viewpoints. After viewing the video given in the "In Conclusion" section, you may have your own ideas about the benefits and losses associated with globalization. In order to briefly review these views, consider the following points: There are clearly a large number of arguments in favor of globalization. It has brought considerable benefits for many countries, enabling them to seemingly maximize their economic potential. The removal of trade barriers has helped millions of people escape from poverty, while multinational companies have used globalization to expand operations, reach new markets, and increase the incomes of their investors. The evidence suggests that globalization has helped countries grow faster, while world trade has increased living standards.

Globalization in Developing Countries

Given the rise in demand for workers who possess skills that post-industrial economies require to remain competitive, job opportunities for those who possess advanced intellectual, analytical, and information-processing capacities have expanded to an unprecedented degree. These expansions provide the policy logic underpinning contemporary discussions on both the shortcomings of industrial education and the need to create a high-skill, high-value labor market. In most developed countries, there is thus growing recognition that education for the future development of knowledge and information-based economic activities and economic production areas needs to be tailored. Moreover, transformations in the institutional environment of all education sectors aimed at these will be essential. Increased access to advanced forms of education has thus become perceived as being indispensable for developed countries in their struggle to adapt to rapidly changing global conditions and developments.

Globalization is associated with increased demand for education in developed countries as companies require more highly skilled people to operate in the global marketplace. However, in many developing countries, wavering to the pressures of globalization and competition from increased trade show that the increased number of job opportunities has not followed. In the long term, investment in education consolidation and improvement of all levels of education from early childhood through to higher education and lifelong learning is essential. In conclusion, greater access to a wider range of high-quality education that ensures high individual potential to improve and retain an ability to adapt and raise the living standards of both countries is a consequence of globalization.

CHAPTER 9

Future of Globalization

One obvious question is whether all this growth in globalization can continue and, if not, what will limit it. Will "real" economic forces (factors of production or costs of basic inputs) lead to a slower growth in the trade in products and the investment in factors of production of different countries, or will inherent social, cultural, political or economic attributes of nations or broader aggregates weaken these cross-border relationships? Some may be what the author may call mythological as globalization has been successful and beneficial. But there are several other "beyond the best" reasons, which is specific strategies for managing the short-run growth of the negative "consequences" and to give the different "roles" to large and small entities within and across societies. Some emphasize the primacy of competitiveness relative to corporate profits while others note that competitiveness is driven by productivity, of which workers, capital, innovation, and a cooperative international environment (a better institutional design) are the key participants.

Every day, globalization in the broadest sense breaks new ground, largely thanks to the advance of technology. It further commodifies goods, services, people, human rights, and the environment. It is also, though not all in one when, fostering democracy, improving access to information, and strengthening freedoms. Globalization policies being simultaneously developed by public and/or private institutions (the state, private interest groups, the international financial organizations, and regional or world financial organizations) are useful for understanding the ever-widening variations of situations brought about by economic, socioeconomic, and socio-geographic globalization. Mass and conflict-centered discontent is likely to continue unless positive policies are assigned to globalization, leading to a universally improving and open society.

Trends and Forecasts

Many economists think that, based on the experiences since the Second World War, the tide of globalization will continue flowing over national borders as countries liberalize and expand their economic policies. Business strategy analysis by groups such as the Boston Consulting Group similarly indicates that the forces pushing towards globalization are likely to continue. Their surveys show companies still expecting sales from foreign affiliates to grow significantly more rapidly than domestic sales. Fully 81 percent of the companies in their 1993 study anticipated annual rates of growth exceeding 10 percent in selling into other foreign subsidiaries and markets over the 1995-2000 period, as against only 36 percent expecting similarly high rates of growth in their domestic businesses. Moreover, it is not only the pace of sales and foreign direct investment which are predictions of globalization. There has been a significant growth in many cross-border transactions including transportation, banking, securities trading, information service and entertainment (through movies, music, television, and printed materials), insurance, advertising, consulting services, and legal services.

The globalization of markets has attracted numerous studies that make various predictions about its development. Much of that interest has arisen, perhaps unsurprisingly, in the context of international business and economics. Nevertheless, a number of academic studies have paid close attention to the process of globalization. These show that the twentieth century was in many ways the century of the multinational corporation, especially in the period since the Second World War. The value of exports of goods and services relative to world GDP rose from about 7 percent in 1913 to about 12 percent in 1950 and about 25 percent in 2001. Again in this period the stock of foreign direct investment rose from equivalent to 61 percent of world GDP in 1913 to about 13 percent in 1950 and about 24 percent in 2001.

CHAPTER 10

Conclusion and Reflections

This presents a detailed case study of globalization. It was designed to probe beneath the surface of students' conceptions of globalization to uncover how they made sense of their place in a globalized world and chose to act or not act in response to the many opportunities and challenges it presents. Throughout the unit, students were encouraged to think critically and construct their own understandings about globalization from a number of sources - academic readings, trade statistics, electronic databases, current events, and multimedia resources.

Our analysis of students' learning has led us to a number of insights about teaching and learning globalization. Although globalization is a complex, often controversial topic that carries with it deep emotional, personal, and interest-based elements, it is accessible to students. Stimulating discussion and personal reflection about globalization can assist with creating a sense of collective identity and common purpose in the classroom. Nevertheless, around this topic - perhaps more than others - teachers need to be alert to the influences of the gender, background, interest, bias, assumptions, and stereotypes of their students on their learning. Even though globalization deals with big ideas and the 'big picture,' many factors associated with place-based forms of identity and local-level activities may limit the ability of particular groups of people to effectively participate in the era of globalization. The ways in which teachers and others are able to promote critical thinking about patterns of participation, equality, fairness, and justice inherently tied to teaching and learning the topic of globalization.